Avoid the

Scams

of

Brokers & Advisors

Ian Sender MBA
The Pimps of Wall Street

IAN Books

An IAN Books paperback

Published by
IAN Books
41 Watchung Plaza, B242
Montclair, NJ 07042

Copyright © 2018 IAN Books

All rights reserved. No part of this book or its Interactive Internet CD can be reproduced, transmitted in any form or by any means, electronic or mechanical, including photocopying, recording, or by any information storage and retrieval system, without the written permission of the publisher.

Cover photo: Staff Sgt. Jeffrey Rios by Staff Sgt. Joy Dulen

Special sales for educational use by nonprofits.
IANBooksEditor@yahoo.com

ISBN-13: 9781726328029

ISBN-10: 1726328023

Library of Congress Control Number: 2018956549

IAN Books at Amazon.com

Wealth Without Wall Street:
Buy Direct -- Avoid the Commissions, Fees, Loads

The Insiders' Guides to Buying Discount Financial Services:
Buy Direct and Save $3,000 Every Year

Drop Your Insurance:
Buy Only What You Need

Create Financial Freedom Using Your Wealth Reserve™:
Fix your financial life

The Simple Financial Life:
How to get what you want without going into debt and living paycheck to paycheck

Build Wealth Without Extra Money or Time:
You don't need to budget or get an extra job

Tax-FREE Retirement:
Use the tax code for lifetime income free of tax

The Working Millionaire:
$2,000,000 Tax-FREE Wealth Reserve ™ Self-insure Self-fund

Build Your Own $2,000,000 Tax-FREE Wealth Reserve™:
Self-insure Self-fund your lifestyle

Stop wasting $3,000 every year:
101
financial products *NOT* to buy and why

Avoid the Scams

Wall Street is a 'war' zone — 5

The SCAMS — 11

1. Avoid income taxes. — 20
2. Buffett's investment plan. — 23
3. Compound stock earnings. — 25
4. Buy buy buy investing. — 28
5. Avoid high-fee managers. — 30
6. Liar's Club: 'I can beat the market.' — 31
7. Invest every month automatically. — 34
8. Buy low-cost financial products. — 36
9. Manage investments once a year. — 38
10. Plan spending wisely. — 39

Win the war — 41

The Author — 43

The Miracle of Compounding — 44

Your Investment Plan — 50

Wall Street is a 'war' zone

We must enter this war zone with the protection of knowledge. We could lose all our lifelong savings in one trade. Brokers and advisors have weapons that can 'kill' us financially. They are hidden behind lies, exaggerations, obfuscations and straight-out fraud like faking our signature. Half-truths and our assumptions and greed are also at play. These are our 'soft' underbelly targets.

Usually we are not 'innocent' children. We want great investment returns with little risk. We want great investment ideas that give us something to brag about. We want to feel like we will be rich without the time and effort to achieve it. We don't understand compounding and how investments work. We give a total stranger our money without finding out about them or their firm. Sometimes we give them every cent we have without knowing a thing about the thing we bought.

We think that because the broker or advisor is well-known or their employer runs cool advertisements they must be trustworthy. We think that we could never be cleaned out because our government regulates them. We think that if it came to it we could sue them for our losses.

I submit that investing with a Wall Street broker or advisor is DANGEROUS unless we do our homework. I have been a financial services executive for over 20 years. I was a managing director of sales units of securities firms. I know first hand that there is little oversight of the people who deal with your money. I know that there is little being done to assure you that the people you are dealing with are acting in your best interests.

Let's look at just one example of what I am talking about. Former Morgan Stanley broker was accused of 'churning' an account held by the late founder of Home Shopping Network. After the arbitrator FINRA awarded the estate of Roy M. Speer $34 million, the broker left and was hired by a new firm. They praised her work as "one of the financial services industry's most successful women advisors."

In 2016, she and her former Morgan Stanley branch manager were found to be jointly liable for unauthorized trading, breach of fiduciary duty/constructive fraud, negligence, negligent supervision and unjust enrichment. The arbitrators also found that Morgan Stanley violated a Florida law against exploitation of vulnerable adults. Wow.

I don't know who will pay the award. However, the point is this broker is only now under 'investigation' by the regulator and her new firm is already setting her up with their clients (maybe you). The new employer is claiming she "will be fully vindicated." They checked her out: "Throughout her career, [she] has demonstrated an unwavering commitment to her clients' best interests." As you can see from her record with regulators, the broker has worked for brand-name firms for years.

I don't know what has happened in this situation. What lessons can we learn about the particulars of this possible SCAM? First, it is alleged that the broker and client were involved romantically. Personal involvement creates undue influence. Second, unauthorized trading, breach of fiduciary duty /constructive fraud' means the regulator found the broker had generated commissions without good reason. The estate claimed the broker did not have permission to trade on their own.

Every broker and advisor needs your permission for each transaction or permission to move your money when they want to. Most brokerage firms require a manager or compliance officer to agree with the activity after checking it. The security sold must be licensed for sale by the state and federal governments. The broker has to have a particular license to sell that kind of licensed security.

The BrokerCheck is always a first stop in gaining knowledge for your protection from Wall Street. This broker now works for Pinnacle Investments but it is not clear which one of 5 firms this one is. Checking a listing in FL shows Tampa Bay must have an office for the broker. This broker will have another FINRA arbitration in November to settle her claims that she was framed.

The message here is that even if we win an arbitration award, we may have to wait a long time to collect. Maybe never. The recent report by the arbitrator FINRA, says 71% are settled before the award. Usually when we don't get paid it is simply that the broker or firm is no longer part of FINRA. They may have changed their name or state and is acting illegally.

This example provides us with a start to avoid SCAMS.

Our Checklist:
1. BrokerCheck and other sources of information.
2. Confirm the salesperson has authorization to trade for you.
3. When you have a question, write to your local compliance officer OSJ Office of Supervisory Jurisdiction.
(more below)

I know you will be more careful when you work with your broker or advisor AFTER you review all the SCAMs in the next chapter. If you have been burned before, you might chose to leave your broker or advisor and go with the alternative I am proposing in the following chapters. I have come to the conclusion after being in the business for over 20 years that you will be more successful using Warren Buffett's advice. He is not paid to take your profits.

Warren Buffett, the most successful investor of our lifetime, just proved that there is only *One Decision* you need to make to reach your lifetime goals. He bet $1 million on a *One Decision* strategy against a Wall Street guru with 5 different strategies.

He beat them all. It is simple, he says.

"A very low-cost index is going to beat a majority of the amateur-managed money or professionally-managed money"

A recent study of investments showed that when you pay less, you earn more. Another study showed that over a lifetime of investing with 2% fees, you may give up 63% of your potential nest egg.

Buffett thinks the wealthy don't follow his advice because they think they are smarter than everyone else. But a business person realizes that it is impossible to pick the next Apple or Google. Just like most people know they will not win the lottery no matter how many tickets they buy.

What most people don't realize is that it is the Miracle of Compounding that makes and keeps the rich, rich. Buffett says:

My wealth has come from a combination of living in America, some lucky genes and
compound interest.

You can earn $1,000,000 with $250 a month over time in a low-cost index or just $208,000 with an advisor account averaging 3.79%. So why don't most of us take Buffett's advice and use index funds? The reason: we believe the Wall Street hype or we never learned about them. No one taught us. Our schools never taught us. Most of our parents couldn't teach us either. Even now pre-retirees lack vital knowledge to fix their shortfall.

The *One Decision* strategy is not used because we never learned that the stocks of the 500 largest firms are the *safest* investment we can own for the LONG-TERM. We never learned that bank accounts are only safe for the SHORT TERM. We never learned that the average return of a low-cost index of the largest 500 stocks is over 11% over time. We never learned that this is not just a guess by academics but a reality available to everyone no matter how much or little we have to invest.

Look at the oldest and most successful index fund anyone can buy: Vanguard 500 Index Fund. The cost is 85% LESS than comparable funds from brokers. You own very profitable companies like Apple, Google and Amazon. Since 1976, you would have earned 11% a year. If you had invested just $250 a month in this one fund since '76 you would have about $1,111,000. Compounding earned $1,012,000. You spent $99,000 over time.

Your account *balance* would have gone up 32% and down 37% but you still would have reached your goal because you did not sell your assets: *fund shares*. Not many brokers or money managers could have helped you there—only Buffett has consistently beaten the index over time with about 19% a year since 1965.

This is your *One Decision* investment move—just have the fund trustee at Vanguard or other low-cost fund debit $250 a month from your checking automatically, and *voilà,* $1 million. You do *nothing else* if you want to reach your money targets over time. If you or your advisor sell or stop buying *shares* you lose the compounding factor. If your salesperson takes any fees greater than 0.04% (Vanguard drops your fee 70% with a $10,000 balance), you are giving them your money for no benefit to you.

The very profitable financial industry has kept this strategy secret for over 40 years. Only 5 states may make this information available to high schoolers in a money course. In the past, you had to use a stock broker to buy stock *shares*. They required a large purchase. And the brokers had to keep moving your money around to generate commissions and fees to earn a living.

Vanguard changed all that. John Bogle, the founder,

realized that without high costs, investors could earn more by paying less. Vanguard sells fund *shares* directly to us and the *shares* are bought at cost since the fund is owned by us. It is an actual co-op like farm co-ops, buying large quantities of supplies for farmers without an owner's profit.

We don't need expensive brokers, advisors or agents to create an efficient financial plan. In fact, their high-cost products can take over HALF of our accumulations. All we need is TIME and a plan.

We buy only what we need at discount prices. We don't pay high costs: fees, commissions, charges, expense ratios, bookkeeping, or trading. Over time, the stock market provides 10-12% returns a year. Now we don't have to pay 1-3% a year in order to grow our money. We don't give up over 50% of our earnings:

$3,000 per year @11%   for 33 years = $1,111,000
$3,000 per year @11-1% for 33 years = $778,768
$3,000 per year @11-2% for 33 years = $613,805
$3,000 per year @11-3% for 33 years = $486,634

With **One Decision**, we can earn 11% on our long-term money and end up with a million dollars or more with one phone call. We do not need an advisor or learn how to pick stocks. That is the fastest way to *lose* money. The average advisor-assisted investor earned just 3.79% instead of the market rate of 11%. Dalbar's QAIB.

'Playing the market' by trading stocks and trying to time the market gyrations is the Loser's Game according to research.

We can't afford hedge funds, offshore tax shelters, and expensive Wall Street money managers taking 1-3% a year. We are not as experienced as Mr Buffett. A plain market index fund beat 92-95% of the returns of "professional" managers, including hedge funds. Stock picking by geniuses only works for a short time.

To earn more, we pay as little as we can. We own stocks of companies with certain characteristics. We Pay Less; Earn More.

Instead of trading stocks, we buy more of them when the price is low and fewer when it is high. No one can time the market successfully in the long run.

We don't pay Wall Street owners the $1.3 Trillion per year revenues they take from clients now. If you think you need financial help, pay for a one-time session from a certified planner, not quarterly fees taking 1-2% of your account every year.

Your current advisor is costing you real money. The average return for managed accounts is 3.79%. A low-cost index fund provides 11%. You are giving up 63% of your total potential earnings. You can do better on your own with the *One Decision* strategy. Do you really think an expert at selling knows anything about what will happen to a security or the market in the next hour, week or year? No they don't know or they wouldn't be in sales.

Low-cost stock mutual funds are our *only* viable long-term asset over time. Other assets have lower or more volatile returns. If you have 10 years until you need the money, stocks give you the power to beat inflation as well as all other investments over time.

Selling and buying stocks kills *compounding* – the Buffett strategy for wealth: Vanguard's 500 index return: 11.02% since 1976. All we have to do is buy and keep buying low-cost funds.

I will show you how you can grow your investing dollar to a $ million or more. An hour online or by phone is all you need to set up the account. We use a special investment account to eliminate all future taxes on this money too. It is IRS-approved for working people.

You have a TAX-FREE account with no brokerage fees or commissions. You keep ALL your hard-earned money and earnings, including the capital gains taxes others have to pay. The less you pay the more you keep. And no taxes!

The wealthy have figured out how to avoid taxes. For instance, Warren Buffett, with $90 billions, pays only 17% **total tax**: http://www.youtube.com/watch?v=Cu5B-2LoC4s; Mitt Romney only **14%**; John Kerry only **13%** and Apple just **9.8%**. Buffett found that his staff pays **32.9%**—DOUBLE his rate!

You set up a tax-FREE account with the largest mutual fund company. You will have that company's trustee invest your automatic bank debit once a month. You do nothing else—No trading; No market timing; No speculation. It's *TIME, not timing.*

Bogle created the first consumer index fund. You do not need to try to pick the "needle" in the haystack, he says. The chance of your advisor identifying the next Apple or Google is 1 in 19,000 annually. Because there are so many variables that we can't determine as a company grows, it is almost impossible to pick, in advance, the one that beats the market *over time*. We can pick the TIME we spend in the market; not the one blockbuster stock.

The SCAMS

I will expand our checklist of SCAMs. So far we had an example of why you must use BrokerCheck and other sources of information. We have to see if our sales person is licensed to sell the product they offer. The product must be registered too. Each legal security has a CUSIP number. US government bonds are exempt. You are at risk if you are offered 'private placement' securities as hedge funds are prone to use.

A favorite sales tactic is to create a story that you are being given a special opportunity to buy something that is very rare. The problem is that you may never be able to unload that special something. In order to take on this risk, you must do your own homework on the issuer of the security. Is it rare? Is the issuer sound financially? There are no guarantees in financial services no matter how good the story.

For instance, this broker who stole $4 million from his elderly clients told them that the investment would allow them to diversify their portfolios, receive annual investment returns as high as 20%, and give them investment growth potential that was better than the growth they received in their brokerage accounts.

This MA advisor stole $3 million over 6 years by *forging signatures* and convincing clients to make fake tax payments. She sold variable annuities and securities and continued by faking statements and documents. Finally after 6 years one client complained about her balance.

A FL penny stock manipulator was caught after using a relatives $2.8 million to buy and then cancel $3 million worth of a bogus mineral exploration stock. This activity tripled the price in two weeks during which he sold millions of shares to unsuspecting clients. Then he sold his shares, doubling his own money. The SEC fined him $500,000 for this 'pump and dump' SCAM.

This MD advisor was caught using client money to finance his lifestyle changes after promising a guaranteed safe 6% return from an insurance company. Anytime you hear the words "guaranteed" or "safe" from an advisor, call the firm's compliance manager (OSJ) immediately.

This pastor-advisor and his felon friend convinced many property owners to refinance their homes to invest in a pension scheme that was supposed to **give them monthly payments** during their retirement. Victims are suing to recover $100 million from the pair. The scheme bought other people's pensions for a current lump sum. The felon friend has not been located.

Sometimes the SCAM is really an exaggeration of benefits as in an insurance product. These products are complicated – the insurer never loses money. This one is universal life policy and 'uses the performance of market indexes to calculate the interest credited to your policy.' It promises a '15% Indexed Interest Multiplier — which sets [the insurer] apart from all other insurance companies.' What may not be understood by buyers are the 'participation rate, cap rate and floor rate' which lower earnings.

Another advisor was caught offering old-fashioned investments **disguised as innovative digital coin** investments. The coins were supposed to fund oil exploration and drilling in CA. The advisor used fake oil production projections. He promised you could convert your digital coins into equity. He had already been convicted of defrauding penny stock investors.

A well-known bank advisory unit was caught generating "large fees" by improperly encouraging retail customers to trade debt securities known as market-linked investments (MLIs) – which are intended to be held until maturity – before they were mature and investing the proceeds back into more MLIs. This strategy generated returns for the bank while reducing investor profits, the SEC said. You have to understand the product before you buy it. You can NOT assume a well-known bank would NOT sell a security improperly—taking your profits for themselves.

Another well-known bank advisory unit was caught and fined $4 million plus $2 million restitution for failure to accurately consider and describe costs and benefits of variable annuity (VA) exchanges, and for recommending exchanges without a reasonable basis to believe they were suitable for customers. Insurers provide terrific incentives for VA sales. The firm promised the VA had a 'living rider benefit guaranteeing minimum payments to customers and their beneficiary when none existed.'

You could have realized that your new VA charges were higher and you did NOT have this new benefit if you had a law degree and read the 78 page contract. Insurers have contracts that protect them no matter what happens in the future. BE WARY.

This investment advisor subsidiary of BNY Mellon Corp was caught failing to monitor and disclose "trading away" fees charged in its separately managed account wrap program. Trading away, also called "step-out trading," is when portfolio managers execute trades through broker-dealers that do not participate in the firms wrap program. This *triggers more fees* from the 'outside' broker. So you are never told about another fee on top of your annual 'wrap' fee. You don't even see the extra fees "because your account statements and trade confirmations disclosed only the *net* cost per trade, with any transaction costs included in the price of the security."

Most firms print securities' confirmations as *net* because they don't like to print "Your commission, fees or costs" as a line item. Why draw your attention to the costs – you might question it! For instance, when you buy a mutual fund thru your sales person, you are not usually shown these costs:

Sales Loads (including Sales Charge (Load) on Purchases and Deferred Sales Charge (Load))

Redemption Fee

Exchange Fee

Account Fee

Purchase Fee (Although the fee table in Form N-1A does not specifically include "purchase fees," if a fund imposes one, it would be included in the fee table under this heading.

Management Fees

Distribution [and/or Service] (12b-1) Fees

Other Expenses

Total Annual Fund Operating Expenses

Instead you must affirm that you read the 'prospectus' usually over 100 pages of legal protections for the seller. The firms' stance with the regulator is: "Client told us they read it so we are not liable." This is why you must completely understand what you are buying or don't buy it. Your broker or advisor is a sales person not your lawyer. *Caveat Emptor* is the phrase that I and every sales person learns for our licenses. It's just 'tough' if you don't understand.

Usually the sales person doesn't understand completely either.

Maybe we should check what a 'wrap' account really does. The original idea was that you pay one fee for all the transactions done in your account. It was supposed to protect you against 'churning' – over active trading to enhance commissions and fees. Trades are supposed to grow your balance (AUM). In fact a wrap does not include all fees and charges. Your attorney can try to figure out which ones are 'wrapped.' Your 'wrap' fee will reduce your total potential accumulations if you already have a great portfolio. When you don't have activity, you may give up to 63% of potential value over time because your fee compounds just like your investments. You may be paying for very little actual 'advice.'

Active trading and market timing have not been shown to help investors either. As I said above, your broker or advisor is probably costing you real money. The average return for managed accounts is 3.79%. Cost is the best predictor of a successful investment. Over time, a low-cost market index does better. That is why Fidelity and Schwab have begun to offer low-cost index funds to compete with Vanguard's 500 Index which returns 11.04%.

SCAMs abound offering high returns at low risk. This is not possible because there are millions of people seeking high returns at less risk and if there was an investment that produced them, everyone would own that investment.

A registered advisor in CA was caught misleading clients; after promising growth he made risky option trades and lost $thousands. This SCAM did not fool a client who looked at the confirms and the market returns.

This advisor offered higher returns than similar investments would pay. This WA advisor was caught selling unregistered promissory notes without being a broker-dealer or being affiliated with one. The securities in question promised to pay investors annual returns generally ranging from 12% to 13%. They were supposed to fund the "factoring" of accounts receivable in Brazil. Clients gave him $64 million without checking with Brazil.

A NY advisor is facing a 99-count indictment alleging he operated a multimillion-dollar securities fraud scheme. The AG said he defrauded many elderly and near-retirement clients out of their savings by investing their money in his hedge fund without their knowledge or consent. His fund collapsed after losing 92% of its value. He ran the fund himself and told investors they would be "better" off with him. You could easily have seen this as a SCAM since his performance was bad in a bull market and he had no credentials to run a hedge fund.

This LI broker was caught running a $66 million Ponzi SCAM by promising steady returns in foreign currency trading. The firm sent out fictitious account statements listing phony trades and profits. Early investors were paid with later investors' money. When loses began to climb, the game was up. You could have learned this from checking what the statements claimed.

This NY advisor hit the jackpot with a Ponzi scheme. He stole $ millions from a company's pension funds. He ran his advisory service as Executive Compensation Planners. His assets were frozen in June but there is no way to know in advance that your pension was at risk. The website that tracks all company pensions, Brightscope, has little info about his firm. He was registered with a broker-dealer which has many ways for an advisor to be associated with it. There is little information.

Ponzi schemes are usually short-term SCAMs so how did Madoff steal $65 Billions since he had not traded in the market since the early 1990's. While most Ponzis are based on nonexistent businesses, Madoff's brokerage operation was very real. Most Ponzis operate on cash flow—take in $100 and pay out 10-15% to existing investors. Keep the rest. Madoff was a respected presence on Wall Street—he served as the chairman of the board of directors and on the board of governors of the brokerage regulator NASD.

Madoff's 'genius' was that he offered modest but steady returns to an exclusive clientele. The investment method was marketed as "too complicated for outsiders to understand." He was secretive about the firm's business. The ultimate con man. He preferred not to see clients but used feeder firms to entice charities and high net worth individuals (like Mets owner, Wilpon). Madoff had many friends in high places which probably saved him from real audits by the SEC and NASD/FINRA. Madoff is in prison and his clients are receiving partial refunds.

How could you avoid the Ponzi SCAM. I don't know about Madoff. Almost everyone was taken in. One thing that might have tipped you off—if it sounds to good to be true, it probably is not true. Very few brokerage firms that trade with options are consistently successful. Warren Buffett puts his methods on review every quarter so he can prove his firm earns 20% over time. He recently beat 5 hedge fund strategies with his *One Decision* strategy.

Variable annuities are complex securities wrapped up in an insurance policy to provide deferred taxation. They are so complex that securities firms must supervise their sale and resale ('1035 exchange') very closely. Many large firms are fined because they do NOT supervise closely enough. Clients ultimately don't understand what they are buying and usually the product is not 'suitable' for them to buy. However, the commissions and fees are so high sales people and firms can't resist.

In one investigation, the regulator fined a bunch of firms $2.7 million and they agreed to do a better job. However, the onus is still on you and so the regulator mandated you have a "free look" period of ten or more days during which you may terminate your contract without paying any surrender charges and receive a refund for the contract. Once you miss that period the cost of canceling can be 10% or more of your balance. There are other costs and caveats you must learn before you buy. Once you're in it, it is hard to break a contract with a securities firm.

In another regulator action, a brokerage firm violated the short-sale rule and failed to supervise sellers and correct practices going on for 3 years. You may not be affected by the violations but if you short stocks your broker must follow the SHO rules to avoid collapse. Short selling is very risky because you can lose more than your investment. For instance, if you bet that Tesla would fall and it went private, you could lose a lot. If you do short selling, ask the compliance officer (OSJ) if the firm is out of SHO compliance.

Many folks get angry and blame the broker for losing money or not earning enough money—but what if the sales people are not even brokers or advisors. In South Florida, older people are being sold unregistered and bogus investment products at 'retirement' conferences. One group run by a former broker created a $1.2 billion Ponzi scheme that targets the elderly. Sales people are pushing products that promise guaranteed or stable returns to clients. You can easily avoid this group by using BrokerCheck.

Other brokers/advisors have the license and use dinners, fancy offices, convincing arguments and cool charts to convince you to buy into a SCAM that they say many other 'smart' investors already own. Sales people leverage your emotions all the time.

Depending on your advisor's official relationship to clients, you may be defrauded by the advisor because they did not provide you with unbiased advice concerning products offered by their firm. A well-known firm was caught by the SEC for not informing 1,500 of its clients that a product sold by their advisor may not be available at the firm anymore. This may affect its resale value.

This would be like you buying an Edsel car on the last day it was to be sold by Ford forever. Parts would be more expensive and resale may have been at a loss. Of course now some Edsels are collector items for $200,000 and parts are custom made.

If your advisor is a RIA registered investment advisor, they take an oath to act in your best interest. However, this is misleading since they only sell for-profit products offered by their firm. They can't sell a Vanguard fund unless it is attached to an account with fees and charges. Usually RIAs are paid a fee based upon a percentage of your total assets no matter what they did to earn the fees. Brokers are paid via firm fees and trips/bonuses.

Brokers and advisors are supposed to offer you products that are 'suitable' for you—not the 'best' for you. Quite often the seller or firm doesn't know what will happen to the product. For instance, the new law offers tax breaks to the wealthy if they invest in infrastructure projects in areas designated by politicians for development. Real estate firms are starting Opportunity Zone funds so investors can co-own apartment buildings in cities like Detroit and reap unique tax benefits at the same time.

This kind of investment is long-term and complicated. Even your attorney and accountant do not understand how these real estate deals will work out. Will the re-zoning go through local political boards? Will you have time to use the tax advantages promised? You might just consider this kind of investment only if you are in the same situation as the author—President Trump.

We still fall for the simple cold call broker selling a penny stock by making it look like a fast moving-up market. We believe a Hook: Get in before the price reaches highs that make your 10000 shares worth $ millions. This PA broker was caught in a penny stock fraud by cold calling prospective buyers. The brokers did not tell clients they were being paid $ thousands to hype the stock. This type of SCAM is easy to avoid by using BrokerCheck.

Even after this broker was caught in his $ million penny stock SCAM on LI which turned into the movie "Wolf of Wall Street" and book tours, he has not paid back much of the restitution he owes to clients. If you had learned about this SCAM from the earlier movie Boiler Room, you would not be waiting for your refund still. Many people who bring broker complaints to the regulator FINRA end up waiting for their settlement—some forever.

The newest flavor of the month for SCAM creators is the virtual currency ETF or exchange traded fund. Regulators have rejected more proposals from legit manufacturers but that won't stop illegal sales to those open to getting rich quickly. Problem is you will own nothing but the dreams of other gamblers. Those seeking to list the products failed to show how they would "prevent fraudulent and manipulative acts and practices."

Gambling on the price of a electronic blip going up in 'value' is fairly easy to avoid. Hackers can easily empty accounts.

Finally, this broker of major firm with a long-time relationship with now older client was caught 'churning' his account by his daughter and now caretaker. The broker had been selling Exxon in small batches to run up commissions. He made 1,499 unauthorized trades in 2017. He used a margin account (loan from firm) to buy stock without approval. After confronting this top firm, they settled as she was going to arbitration. The firm has not fired the broker. She looked at the confirms.

Apparently the client did not watch the confirms or statements and neither did the firm which should have stopped this broker from 'churning' before it started.

Protect yourself! From these current examples, you can see that using a successful broker or advisor from a brand-named firm will NOT save you from being a victim of SCAM. The insurance that firm's carry like SIPC do not pay you for bad firms or bad representatives. You must be vigilant and here is your checklist:

Our Checklist:
1. BrokerCheck and other sources like investor.gov.
2. Confirm the salesperson has authorization to trade for you.
3. When you have a question, write to your local compliance officer OSJ Office of Supervisory Jurisdiction.
4. Unregistered offerings are putting your money at risk. CUSIP.
5. Are the investment returns within a reasonable range? 2% is the return of US bonds; 11% is the return of the broad market. Here are the 20 year returns of specific market sectors.

6. Is the advisor recommending some plan that is illegal? This may require you to have an attorney check out the deal.
7. Do you completely understand the terms of the deal and what can go wrong? Assumptions change over time. Sellers retire.
8. Make sure you read the SEC warning about variable annuities.
9. Be wary of free dinners, fine talk, great facilities, cool charts: don't stop doing your homework.
10. Any promised returns, "guarantee" or "safe"? Call the OSJ.
11. Beware: Penny stock (less $2) trading is dangerous for client.

As I said at the top, you only have one easy way to protect yourself and I think it is the only way to safely invest for your retirement or any long-term need. Warren Buffett's *One Decision* strategy uses one mutual fund for life and since there is no trading account, there is no broker or advisor to get you into trouble. Since you are not trading—market timing or buying high and selling low, you have a good chance of earning 11%—not the 3.79% that represents the REAL earnings of advisor-advised accounts.

You can avoid the scams since you do not let anyone touch your account. If you need help, you call your mutual fund trustee since you are going to use a tax-FREE trust. You can only earn 10-12% by compounding your earnings. This is the Buffett strategy:

My wealth has come from a combination of living in America, some lucky genes and
compound interest.

You can earn $1,000,000 with $250 a month over time in a low-cost index or just $208,000 with an advisor account averaging 3.79%. So why don't most of us take Buffett's advice?

Hubris: excessive pride or self-confidence: smarter than Buffett

When the best investor of our time wins a bet against 5 hedge funds by using the most popular low-cost mutual fund available to everyone, you take note. Stock pickers and advisor-run funds are not the best investment for us over time. Of course, someone will win the high-return prize for the year. However, most of us realize we are not as smart as Warren Buffett.

I follow Warren Buffett's advice. It's more profitable.

Avoid income taxes

The *One Decision* strategy relies on low-cost funds and compounding. But the *One Decision* strategy works even better when we make our account tax-FREE—no income tax later.

The wealthy have ways we don't have to avoid taxes. Consider the examples above: Buffett pays just **17%**, Romney **14%**, Kerry **13%** and Apple **9.8%**. Most of the top 1% pay far less tax than the average American in terms of income.

If the average middle-class family earns $85,000, they pay about 14% federal, 13% SS/Med/UC/Health, 10% state/local, 4% sales/excise, or over 30% total taxes. As Buffett said, "I pay 17.7% total tax. My office staff pays 32.9%." This does not include pension, insurance and other deductions most Americans also pay.

This is why the wealthy avoid taxes with their own businesses and various tax-advantaged vehicles. In order to become and stay wealthy, people need to have money to invest. The average family has little extra money to build wealth let alone have enough for retirement. They need tax-FREE compounding.

The following graph makes clear that in order to accumulate $1,000,000 from monthly contributions, we must buy and hold the securities of growing companies worldwide AND pay **zero** tax on the growth to *maximize compounding*. We can see clearly that investing in growing company stocks is more likely to get us to our goal in our lifetime than investing in government bonds or a bank savings account. (lower lines)

As your investments grow—especially mutual funds that pay dividends and gains each year—you will not have to pay tax on them because of your special IRS-approved account. Most regular IRAs and pension accounts are tax-DEFERRED *not* tax-FREE. Taxes have to be paid sometime.

Senator William Roth got us this account in 1998. Your Roth IRA allows you to leverage tax-FREE accumulations over time against an immediate tax deduction as with a regular IRA or 401k pension. The benefits can be enormous: if you contributed $250 a month to your low-cost stock mutual funds, you could spend $30,000 tax-FREE for every $3,000 you deposited!

Invest $250 a month, $3000 a year, never pay tax

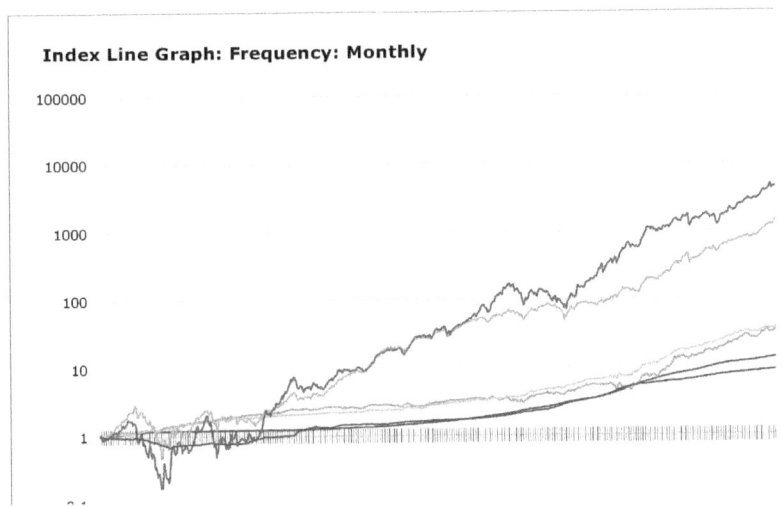

Top line—Small Cap Stocks
2nd line—Large Cap Stocks (S&P 500)
3rd line—US Long-term Corporate Bonds
4th line—Intermediate-term Government Bonds
5th line—US 30 day Government T-bills
6th line—US inflation
Courtesy: Dr. Campbell R. Harvey http://www.duke.edu/~charvey/

Tax-FREE v Taxable

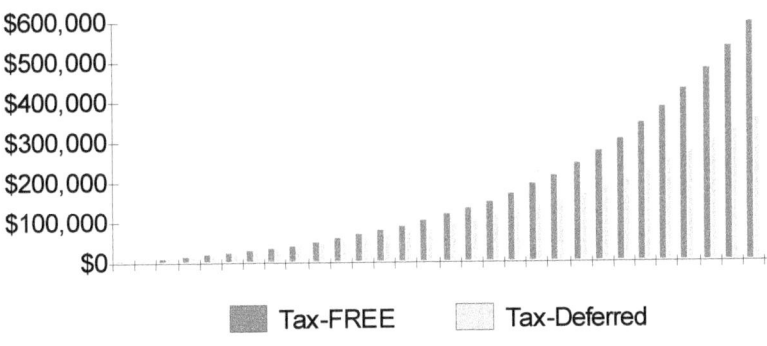

Tax-FREE   Tax-Deferred

The Roth IRA Rules

Contributions:

$5,500 ($6,500 over age 50) each year
Income under $135,000 (2018) single
married $199,000 (2018)

Distributions:

Tax-FREE for contributions.
And Tax-FREE for earnings if
Over age 59 1/2,
Account open 5 years,
Taxable earnings unless
Disabled,
First home ($10,000),
Death

Bonus:

Account can grow tax-FREE for life
Minimum distribution rules don't apply
Heirs don't pay income tax
Account has no maximum

Check with your tax preparer
https://www.irs.gov/pub/irs-pdf/p590a.pdf

Buffett's investment plan

You don't need an advisor. You can manage the rules of your Roth IRA account yourself. The rules are found at https://www.irs.gov/retirement-plans/roth-iras. Your account trustee can answer most questions. You don't need to pay an attorney. All of the large low-cost mutual funds firms are trustees. I will discuss the best firms available below.

You can start this account with any of the firms with no upfront charges. Most charge an annual fee for the bookkeeping. We will consider the specific investment options later. We will use low-cost firms because you will keep more of your own money. You save money when you don't pay Wall Street to 'advise' you.

It is important to pick a trustee with the least costs since over time the annual costs can really destroy your accumulations. For instance, if you use a brokerage firm, you might pay 2-3% of your balance annually. You could give up 63% of your earnings. If both spouses have a low-cost account with contributions of $250 a month for 27 years, they could accumulate $1,000,000. If they use a high-cost broker/advisor, both accounts may hit only $282,000. Depending on earnings of 8-10% and total costs of 2% per year, you could really hurt yourself. You need to watch the costs. Advisors do NOT beat the markets over the long term. Just stick with your *One Decision* plan.

You can open your account at any age as long as you have *earned* income—paper route too. Stock dividends or interest do not count. Any job will do. You don't even need a job requiring a W-2 to prove it. A part-time, weekend or night job will do. Any cash-only work will qualify—even for a child. Accountants recommend that receipts and records be maintained. You could even work for yourself in a home-office business like I do.

Nontaxable distributions from a Roth IRA won't affect your eligibility for student aid either. Later, in retirement, this money won't affect your social security benefits as of the rules today.

The *Miracle of Compounding* works.

Actual client Tom's account, investing $250 a month, 1962-2003

24%	3,720
16%	7,795
12%	12,091
-10%	13,582
24%	20,561
11%	26,153
-8%	26,821
4%	31,013
14%	38,775
19%	49,713
-14%	45,333
-26%	35,766
37%	53,110
24%	69,576
-8%	66,770
6%	73,956
18%	90,809
32%	123,827
-5%	120,486
22%	150,653
21%	185,920
6%	200,255
32%	268,297
19%	322,843
5%	342,135
17%	403,808
32%	536,987
-3%	523,787
31%	690,091
8%	748,538
10%	826,692
2%	846,286
38%	1,172,015
23%	1,445,268
33%	1,926,197
28%	2,469,372
21%	2,991,570
-9%	2,725,059
-12%	2,403,420
-22%	1,874,601
29%	2,412,905

Compound stock earnings

Compounding high earnings is your *best* strategy. The wealthy get richer just by leaving their money invested. They don't work more hours or take more risks. The famous 1% at the top of society take down 23.5% of all income (up from 8.9% 30 years ago). They don't work any harder than you do—*their money does.*

Because of compounding, many millionaires have said, "the first million was the hardest." It takes a working business person about 34 years to grow $250 a month to $1,000,000 using tax-advantaged investments. However, it only takes 7-9 years to double their money to $2 million. Investors in stock funds, earning 10-12% on average, can double it again to $4 million in less than 10 years without adding new money. Their tax-advantaged accounts make it easier to reach their goal. It is compounding that makes it happen—not Wall Street 'advice' for the fees.

Compounding of high earnings means that we make money on our last period's accumulations. The progression looks like the client's account values on the previous page. Notice that our balance can double in a couple of good years. This happens because we are adding up to 38% of the previous year's balance not because we add $3,000. We are making money on top of our money with no extra effort on our part. During this 40 year period, this client 'lost' share value some years. In fact, they lost 14% and then 26% back to back, but then made 37% and 24%.

Wealthy people don't panic. They have learned that compounding over the long-term is the only way they can build wealth. There are no successful get-rich-quick schemes for the investors. To reach their goal, they know there will be setbacks. No business grows steadily upward all the time. They have seen the losses before and they don't sell their assets in a panic.

We will buy <u>assets that "grow by themselves.</u>" We will have security because our ***<u>purchasing power</u>*** will grow over time. We begin with a fund with 500 large company stocks. We earn 10-12%. Some go on to buy all ten Vanguard funds reducing the market ups and downs. We still buy the shares because their value goes up over time. We buy the shares monthly and ***the number of our shares*** never ***goes down.***

The Vanguard Top Ten

2017 Total Return	Fund	Long-term Return	Longevity
21.7%	*500 Index*	*11.1%**	*since 1976*
3.2%	Energy	10.7%	since 1984
17.9%	Extended Market	10.9%	since 1987
19.6%	Health	16.5%	since 1984
42.9%	International Growth	10.8%	since 1981
29.5%	PRIMECAP	13.9%	since 1984
16.1%	Small Cap Index	10.7%	since 1960
10.2%	Wellesley Income	9.9%	since 1970
19.1%	Windsor	11.5%	since 1958
16.8%	Windsor II	10.8%	since 1985
19.7%	Average	11.7%	

*Average Annual Returns as of 12/31/17.

This kind of security comes from our regular contributions ... and patience. The miracle of compounding works its magic on the fund shares when we give it TIME. The wealthy give their **assets** time to compound. They don't take them out and they try not to pay tax every year on the gains. They maintain their contribution schedule because each $100 added is worth $1,000 to them later. They use the compound interest calculator so they know the future value: moneychimp.com/calculator/compound_interest_calculator.htm.

Most people who become wealthy have to wait for years of slow growth in their account. It took client Tom 21 years to get to $150,000. Then it took only 14 years to get to a $1,172,015. After only 4 years, it became $3,000,000. Shortly thereafter he "lost" over a million dollars! He never lost his shares since he never sold.

This client stuck with it and was successful in reaching the goal but there are many who do not. Most people who are not wealthy already, have a hard time believing it can happen with only their *patience*. They just don't have the experience of how compounding works to keep faith in its outcome eventually.

Once an account becomes sizable, we don't need to add contributions to it--usually, by the time we stop regular employment. Some people continue to work after age 65 because they love what they do and want to continue. Obviously, they don't need to work. The **miracle of compounding** does the work then.

The annual returns of growing companies

2016 Total Return	Fund	Long-term Return	Longevity
11.9%	500 Index	10.9%*	since 1976
33.1%	Energy	10.9%	since 1984
16.1%	Extended Market	10.7%	since 1987
-9.0%	Health	16.4%	since 1984
1.7%	International Growth	10.0%	since 1981
10.7%	PRIMECAP	13.4%	since 1984
18.3%	Small Cap Index	10.7%	since 1960
8.1%	Wellesley Income	9.9%	since 1970
12.5%	Windsor	11.3%	since 1958
13.4%	Windsor II	10.7%	since 1985
11.7%	Average	11.5%	

*Average Annual Returns as of 12/31/16.

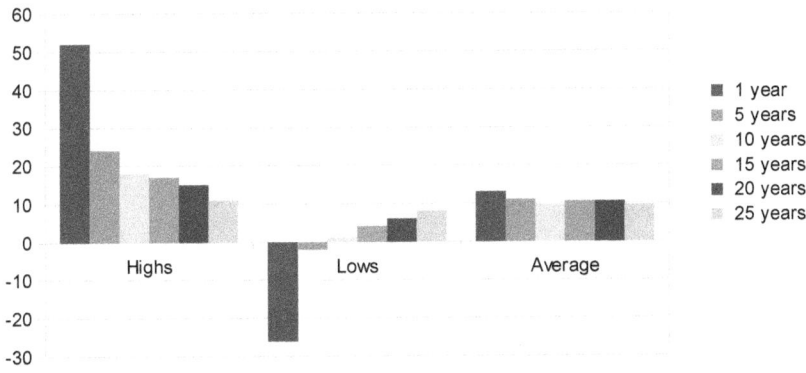

Range of annual returns of stocks, 1950 – 2000

Buy buy buy investing

When we develop the *habit* of investing, we take our emotions out of the process. We, as a silent partner, must learn to live with the market downs. We need to think of this account as our stake in growing businesses as the number of shares grow. See page 13.

It is easier to be patient if we make contributions automatic. Like the Social Security contributions we make every payday, the contributions come out of our bank automatically. We can have the Roth IRA trustee debit our checking account automatically every month. Businesses grow in spurts. We must hold on to our *shares*.

As one client told us, "I never see the deduction, so I never miss it." Of course this client has already identified the $250 he has committed to his $1,000,000 future. He took our advice and went through his spending on financial services. He used our Guides to find the $250 a month he was wasting on products and services he would never use or need. In our amazon.com/Insiders-Guides-Discount-Financial-Services/ you will find **"tricks of the trade"** that we insiders use to buy directly from high quality manufacturers for less.

It's easy to say **I will start later.** Starting 5 years later means ending up with HALF the amount we were shooting for. It is hard to believe that missing that $250 a month for 5 years or $15,000 can reduce our total from $600,000 to $300,000.

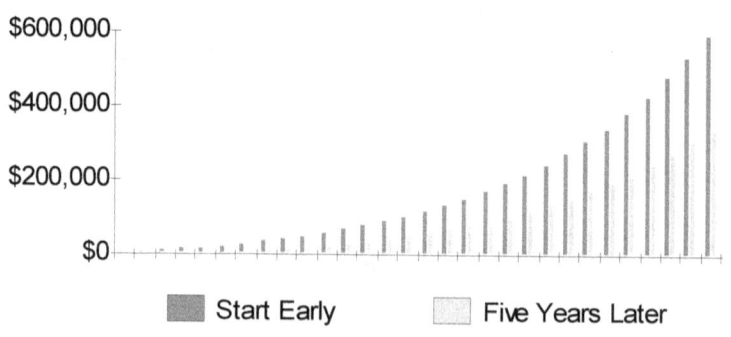

The Value of Starting Early

Your investment plan over time

$2,000 Annual Stock Market Investment 1950- '70- '80- '90- 2013

Year	Returns	Balance	Balance	Balance	Balance	Balance
		$2,000				
1950	31%	$2,620				
1951	24%	$5,729				
1952	18%	$9,120				
1953	-1%	$11,009				
1954	52%	$19,773				
1955	31%	$28,523				
1956	5%	$32,049				
1957	-11%	$30,304				
1958	43%	$46,194				
1959	12%	$53,978				
1960	1%	$56,538				
1961	26%	$73,757				
1962	-8%	$69,697				
1963	24%	$88,904				
1964	16%	$105,449				
1965	12%	$120,342				
1966	-10%	$110,108				
1967	24%	$139,014				
1968	11%	$156,526				
1969	-8%	$145,844	2,000			
1970	4%	$153,757	2,080			
1971	14%	$177,563	4,651			
1972	19%	$213,681	7,915			
1973	-14%	$185,485	8,527			
1974	-26%	$138,739	7,790			
1975	37%	$192,813	13,412			
1976	24%	$241,568	19,111			
1977	-8%	$224,082	19,422			
1978	6%	$239,647	22,707			
1979	18%	$285,144	29,155	2,000		
1980	32%	$379,030	41,124	2,640		
1981	-5%	$361,978	40,968	4,408		
1982	22%	$444,053	52,421	7,818		
1983	21%	$539,724	65,850	11,879		
1984	6%	$574,228	71,921	14,712		
1985	32%	$760,621	97,575	22,060		
1986	19%	$907,519	118,494	28,632		
1987	5%	$954,995	126,519	32,163		
1988	17%	$1,119,684	150,367	39,971		
1989	32%	$1,480,623	201,125	55,402	2,000	
1990	-3%	$1,438,144	197,031	55,680	1,940	
1991	31%	$1,886,589	260,731	75,560	5,161	
1992	8%	$2,039,676	283,749	83,765	7,734	
1993	10%	$2,245,843	314,324	94,342	10,708	
1994	2%	$2,292,800	322,651	98,268	12,962	
1995	38%	$3,166,824	448,018	138,370	20,647	
1996	23%	$3,897,654	553,522	172,656	27,856	
1997	33%	$5,186,540	738,844	232,292	39,709	
1998	28%	$6,641,331	948,281	299,894	53,387	
1999	21%	$8,038,430	1,149,839	365,291	67,019	
2000	-9%	$7,316,791	1,048,174	334,235	62,807	
2001	-12%	$6,447,855	925,203	296,223	57,095	
2002	-22%	$5,024,437	722,291	232,316	46,035	
2003	29%	$6,459,474	930,787	301,119	61,730	
2004	11%	$7,164,483	1,034,274	336,099	70,664	
2005	5%	$7,512,677	1,084,540	352,433	74,098	
2006	15%	$8,694,884	1,259,259	412,409	90,450	
2007	5%	$9,163,538	1,327,133	434,638	95,325	
2008	-39%	$5,601,431	813,388	268,074	60,754	
2009	27%	$7,116,358	952,155	342,993	79,699	
2010	15%	$8,186,112	1,097,278	396,742	93,954	
2011	2%	$8,347,378	1,118,894	404,558	95,805	
2012	16%	$9,666,264	1,295,679	468,478	110,942	
2013	32%	$12,759,468	1,710,296	618,390	146,443	
Avg.	12%	12%	11%	13%	11%	

IAN, LLC © 2014   1/2/14   TheInsidersGuides.com   10

Ibbotson Associates **Stocks average 11.4% per year, bonds 5%, CDs 3%.** Stocks have gone up as much as 54% and as low as –43% in 1 year, up to 28% or down to –12% in 5 years, up 20% or down 0% in 10 years, up 18% or up 3% in 20 years. Short term bonds have gone up 14% or up 0% in 1 year, up 11% or up 0% in 5 years, up 9% or up 0% in 10 years, up 10% or up 1% in 20 years.

Avoid "high-fee managers"

"In every single time period and data point tested, *low-cost funds* beat *high-cost* funds."

According to an unbiased Morningstar study, low-cost funds beat high-cost funds, PERIOD. However, the myth of Wall Street is that you must pay more for good performance. Warren Buffett's mentor, Benjamin Graham, advised: "buy financial products like we buy "groceries, … not perfume."

The best predictor of your investing and wealth-building success is **low cost**. When we subtract the costs of buying and maintaining investments, we give up a lot of the gains. A stock fund that reflects the overall market is called an index fund. This kind of fund costs only 0.04% ($4 per $10,000). Our account will compound at or near the 10-12% trend over time.

The chart below makes it clear. Over time, the advisor costs we pay each year will cut our total accumulation by up to 63%. Instead of compounding at 10-12% annually on average, some people give up 1.5-3% of the earnings on their money to the middle person. They end up with less.

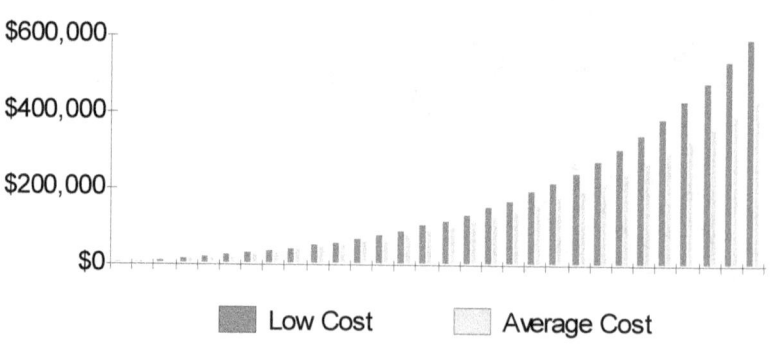

Low-cost index funds beat 95% of funds with a stock-picking manager. Wall Street takes $ 1.3 Trillion of our money in fees.

Liar's Club: 'I can beat the market'

Liar's Poker is a game author Michael Lewis says traders play when they get bored. It involves bluffing. But when your advisor or money manager does it to you, it's fraud. When retail customers don't know how and where to invest properly, sales people make up stories. They don't lie exactly; they mislead. Sales people only survive if they separate you from your money or your potential earnings. Fact: You need a plan that takes only one hour to follow.

Picking **individual** stocks as a strategy is not likely to work for us. Professional managers and day traders have had limited success over time. Our strategy is to build wealth as a silent partner in growing global companies. Since it is unlikely that we (or anyone else) will be able to pick the next Google or Apple, we invest in a large group of firms. We do not need to fear picking the wrong one or picking one at the wrong time. As the founder of the largest mutual fund firm, John Bogle, says: "Don't look for the needle. Buy the haystack." This is a proven successful strategy.

A mutual fund manager advertises that their fund has "beaten" the market and so we pay 1.5-3% of our assets every year. Over time we find that while the stock market index rose **11.06%**, we earned only **3.79%** annually. In this way, costs can take 63% of our returns over time. Each time they sell and buy, we give up some of our compound earnings. Plus we pay fees and taxes.

When young investors begin investing, they cannot buy all 10 Vanguard funds listed above at once with $250 per month. Vanguard has minimums on all funds so they can keep their expenses low for everyone.

There are two ways to start our Roth IRA account. The easiest way is to save $250 a month in our savings account until we have the $1,000 minimum for Vanguard's entry fund: STAR #56. We can open the Roth IRA by phone or online: STAR minimum is $1,000. Most Vanguard funds need $3,000 to start. We can keep contributing to the STAR fund until we have $3,000 for the 500 Index and then $3,000 for the Extended Market funds and eventually all 10 funds. Vanguard is at 800.551.8631.

The second way to begin is to open a Roth IRA at TIAA, the world's largest pension company, primarily for educational and research institutions. Low expenses and low initial contributions make TIAA an organization we can stay with. TIAA 800.842.2888.

At TIAA we can make application and begin immediately with an automatic monthly contribution of $100 or more from our bank account. We can follow how the assets grow by themselves. TIAA has two funds that provide us with the diversity of companies worldwide: TIAA Equity Index and TIAA International Equity.

Request a prospectus (owner's manual) for each fund you will be using at Vanguard or TIAA. Both mutual fund firms have experienced salaried representatives that provide accurate information about accounts and funds. Both offer low-cost index funds that hold a broad representation of the market returns of 10-12%. This is a building block to accumulating wealth.

Both firms are focused on you, not on profits.

Our strategy is to buy mutual funds with stocks of growing companies worldwide. No Wall Street guru can predict the future winners. Most can't do better than 50%—a flip of the coin. Your investments provide long-term growth of 10-12% annually on average with the benefit of avoiding single company or industry failures. It provides exposure to new growth potential around the world with less risk than holding one company, one sector, or one country. Some years our account is up 33% and some years down 22%. However, we double our money every 7-9 years *over time.*

How does your investment grow? Time is the key. Take as example your payday contributions to Social Security. A couple pays in 6.2% of salary. It is matched by the employer. Baby Boomers who made average salaries all their lives are now taking benefits of about $1,500 each--$36,000 a year. Because benefits are pegged to inflation, they may receive $1,260,000 during the rest of their lives. However, SS contributions are NOT invested in the stock market index.

Our investments earn 10-12% a year in an index earning much more than SS contributions. It is TIME that makes wealth.

It is the amount we KEEP that matters!

Monthly	Accumulation at 12% per year								
	5	10	15	20	25	30	35	40	45	50
$100	$8,167	$23,004	$49,958	$98,925	$187,884	$349,496	$643,095	$1,176,477	$2,145,469	$3,905,834
$200	$16,334	$46,008	$99,916	$197,850	$375,768	$698,992	$1,286,190	$2,352,954	$4,290,938	$7,811,668
$300	$24,501	$69,012	$149,874	$296,775	$563,652	$1,048,488	$1,929,285	$3,529,431	$6,436,408	$11,717,502
$500	$40,835	$115,020	$249,790	$494,625	$939,420	$1,747,480	$3,215,475	$5,882,385	$10,727,346	$19,529,169

...

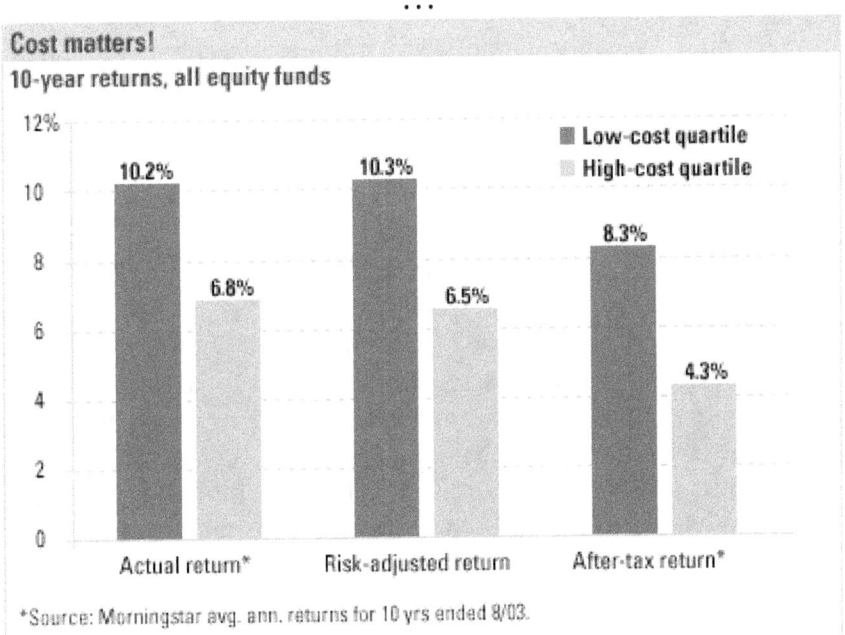

Cost matters!
10-year returns, all equity funds

Low-cost quartile: Actual return 10.2%, Risk-adjusted return 10.3%, After-tax return 8.3%
High-cost quartile: Actual return 6.8%, Risk-adjusted return 6.5%, After-tax return 4.3%

*Source: Morningstar avg. ann. returns for 10 yrs ended 8/03.

Invest every month automatically

We need to find at least $250 per month to invest in order to build our account. We can build wealth by following the strategy outlined in the previous chapters, but we need to have at least 10% of income available to invest. In my experience, it doesn't matter how much people earn, most say they don't have the money to invest for their future. "Today is hard enough," they complain.

Yes, that may well be, but if we don't find the $250, for example, we won't have a very happy tomorrow. We have to go back to our goal. We want to build wealth: accumulating $1,000,000 over time. Based on the way wealth compounds, we need to invest at least $250 a month, every month. We need to be consistent for the **miracle of compounding** to work.

A Spending Plan is a way to set priorities for our regular spending. We can accumulate $1 million to accomplish all that we want to do in life by using just 10 percent of our income to buy assets that "grow by themselves." We don't run the firms we own.

Using a Spending Plan is **like brushing your teeth**—it's a habit that isn't that difficult to learn—then it is automatic. Our Spending Plan must include what we need to function now and in the future. Like building a business, it takes planning and following the steps we talked about so far.

Some investors include the $250 in their automatic bill payment or have the trustee debit their account automatically. Others set up family goals and decide to put a certain amount in a separate account for each goal. In this way, they keep the wealth building process in the forefront of their monthly bill payments.

Whatever way works for you. The important thing is to change the status of wealth building from a vague future desire to a monthly habit. "Set it and forget it" is the theme of investing.

Most people find that the easiest way is to set up an automatic debit of their checking account by the trustee at the time of the application for the Roth IRA. If we are using a Roth 401k or an employer account, we set up the retirement account with automatic contributions. We are less likely to quit if a trustee debits monthly.

Some people are successful by making a written plan. They

have some idea of how much they will need at some time in the future. The account is set up as a Roth IRA so the **contributions** are not taxed when used before age 59.5. After that age, there are no taxes at all—EVER.

Another benefit of using a Spending Plan is that we become focused on how we spend our money. We are more inclined to buy only what we need. For financial services, we 'insiders' compiled the *The Insiders Guides* for each area—insurance, securities, etc. They provide an easy way to save $3,000 or more on financial products we already use. This is where we buy discount products.

We can't build wealth by spending more than we earn. Building wealth takes patience and commitment to contributing to our investment business every month. Some people don't try to be disciplined investors. They let the trustee debit the $250 or 10% every month so they can't fail to become a millionaire.

Are you paying too much?

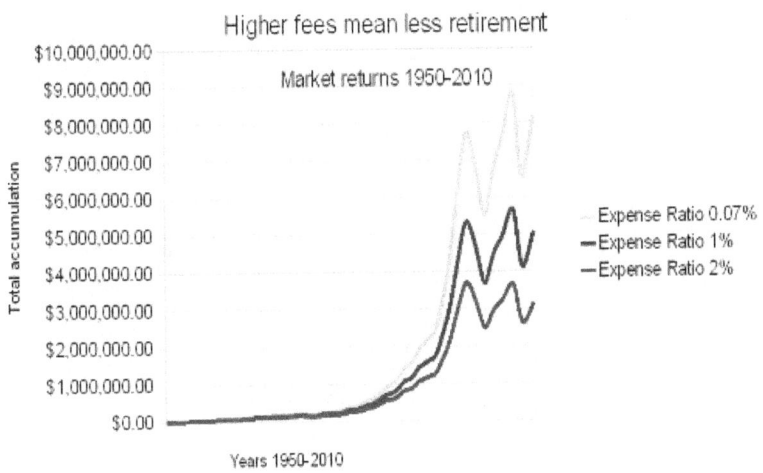

Buy low-cost financial products

John Bogle invented the low-cost mutual fund cooperative structure that allows us to accumulate stock earnings at cost—No middle person or profit firm to take a large chunk of our earnings. It is not picking stocks but *time* that builds wealth. It is easy to build wealth if we already have a pile of money. But how do we capture that first $500,000, that $250,000, or even that first $50,000? It comes from buying assets that 'grow by themselves.' It takes time for the companies we own through your fund to produce earnings. As <u>Buffett just proved</u>, the easiest way to make sure we reach our goal of a million dollars is to buy low-cost.

But where do we get the $250 a month? The best way is to "REDIRECT" the **cash we already spend** on things we really don't need or can buy for less. This is how millionaires stay millionaires. They don't over pay!

Most working people waste $3,000 or more each year on financial services. We must shop for financials like we shop for groceries: buy the house brand and use discounts. For instance, the difference between paying full price for a new car and a 3-year-old model can be 40% or more.

Buy for every financial need for less:
Auto insurance: save $400 or more EVERY year by changing/dropping some benefits we don't need.

Home insurance: save $200 or more EVERY year by changing one limit.

Life insurance: save $1,000 or more EVERY year by using direct to consumer term insurer.

Mutual funds: save $2-3,000 EVERY year by using low-cost providers.

Bank: save $120 EVERY year by using a low-cost provider of the benefits we usually use. <u>Credit Union</u>.

Mortgage: save $2,000 on closings and lower interest rates.

Investments: earn 15-30% *guaranteed* just by paying off credit cards.

Low-cost mutual funds: save up to 63% over time.

Tax refund: Averages $3,022 and usually spent.

Using our ***The Insiders' Guides to Buying Discount Financial Services: Buy Direct and Save $3,000 Every Year***, we can redirect $250 a month without having to give up anything. We don't need to tighten our belt or make a budget. We can give up things we would not benefit from anyway.

Best example: MetLife charged $983 for a $300,000 30-year **term policy**. This same $300,000 benefit was sold by Savings Bank Life Insurance for $384 a year. Their financial strength ratings are A+ and their underwriting requirements are the same. The difference, $599, over 30 years is $17,970. If invested, this difference can add $175,000 to OUR **account**.

This strategy—to cut out the middle people who are taking our money with little benefit to us—makes sense and works! But the most important part of our strategy is keep investing: *buying more shares of mutual funds when they are 'on sale.'*

2011 Total Return	Fund	Long-term Return*	Longevity
1.97%	500 Index	10.36%	since 1976
-1.74%	Energy	12.71%	since 1984
-3.73%	Extended Market	9.96%	since 1987
11.45%	Health	16.30%	since 1984
-13.68%	International Growth	10.50%	since 1981
-1.84%	PRIMECAP	12.79%	since 1984
-2.80%	Small Cap Index	10.26%	since 1960
9.63%	Wellesley Income	10.16%	since 1970
-4.00%	Windsor	11.00%	since 1958
2.70%	Windsor II	10.18%	since 1985
0.00%	Average	11.42%	

*Average Annual Returns as of 12/31/11.

We must ignore what others are doing when some markets fall because we are gaining more shares NOT cashing in at panic prices. Just remember George Bailey's talk during the 1929 panic:

Potter isn't selling. Potter's buying! And why? Because we're panicky and he's not. That's why. He's pickin' up some bargain. Now, we can get through this thing all right. We've, we've got to stick together, though. We've got to have faith in each other. ***It's a Wonderful Life***

Manage investments once a year

"We continue to make more money when *snoring* than when active."

Warren Buffett gave us this advice. As the most successful investor of our day we should listen. He is making it clear that we should NOT touch our investments very often. We buy shares of the top companies and hold them all our lives—selling them only for our retirement income.

Wall Street makes money on transactions. So don't trade. We ignore the market and keep buying so we end up with $1 million. When the market is down we keep our mind on the graph on p. 17. We have to remember Warren Buffett's advice and hold on to stocks/stock funds. In fact, Mr Buffett says "**our favorite holding period is forever.**" http://www.berkshirehathaway.com/letters/1988.html

Even if the market drops; it will rise. It fell 22% in 2002 and rose 29% in 2003. We only have to look at our tax-FREE account once a year. We make sure we are making contributions to the specific mutual fund that is down for the year. We don't 'rebalance.'

When we first started investing, we use the STAR Index. After we had accumulated enough to buy the 500 Index ($3,000), we trade shares of the STAR Index and buy it. We keep investing into the 500 Index until we have the minimum for the next one. We repeat this pattern until we have the minimum in each. Then we add to the one that is down for the year. Repeat each year.

As we accumulate the minimum for each fund, then transfer into the next one, we do not need to pay tax on the sale because we are using a tax-FREE Roth IRA. This is part of the **miracle of compounding**. After accumulating a large proportion of our goal, adding the $250 per month does not matter to the outcome. We can borrow to pay for cars, vacation, other goals. For instance, our client whose account is shown on page 13 took $25,000 for a used luxury car in the year the account hit over half a million. His account total did not suffer long term.

Managing investments once a year is wise advice. Our tax-FREE account does not require us to hire an advisor to manage it.

We have the *power of compounding* so we don't need advisors.

Plan spending wisely

We own the 10 funds to build wealth. We have learned to be patient and accumulate $1,000,000 or more. We have paid back any amounts that we borrowed to pay cash for large purchases. We have been fortunate that the historical averages of market returns have produced the accumulations we set as our goals.

NOW WHAT?

Now we can take 6-8% out of the account each year and pay no income taxes. As of 2018, most states follow the IRS code on our **account**, a Roth IRA. https://www.irs.gov/retirement-plans/roth-iras

Many people move 60% of their money into a balanced fund like the Wellesley Income fund. It has produced over 9% per year on average since 1970. They created a retirement spending plan that assured them of that monthly income of a fixed dollar amount with this Guide. amazon.com/Your-Retirement-Spending-Plan-enough.

We have created our $1,000,000 nest egg in order to provide the same buying power as we have today because of inflation. I am assuming that most working families will need at least $50,000 a year to live on in retirement. We don't know what will happen to Social Security by 2034. We don't know what employer pensions might look like by then. I am assuming that inflation will continue so planning is crucial to success in retirement.

Inflation will make the goods we buy now for $50,000 cost about $80,000. If Social Security or employer pensions can add to our basic income, that is fine. But we don't want to count on them. If there is a bad year like 2008, we are not taking money out of our growth funds at a bad time. The balanced fund has bonds which have traditionally been less volatile.

The funds we have listed above include some of the most consistent low volatility returns over time. Since our account is not taxable, there are no taxes when we take our monthly income later. We may not have to pay tax on our other income like Social Security and/or our qualified retirement funds. The gains on our account are tax-FREE after age 59.5. Unlike pensions and annuities, this account is tax-FREE. We pay $99,000 ($3,000 for 33 years) and $901,000 is FREE of tax.

The Keys to Wealth

1. **Costs matter**: Broker/advisor cost 1% to 3% every year

   If you use a salesperson, costs take HALF your money!
   $3,000 per year @11%   for 33 years = $1,018,177
   $3,000 per year @11-1% for 33 years = $778,768
   $3,000 per year @11-2% for 33 years = $613,805
   $3,000 per year @11-3% for 33 years = $486,634
   www.moneychimp.com/calculator/compound_interest_calculator.htm

2.   Broker/advisor stock-picking does not beat index funds over time. No money manager has been able to beat the markets consistently. No one can forecast the future. http://investa.com/man-vs-machine-the-great-stock-showdown-wall-street-journal-05-10-13/

3. **Compounding** creates investment success; NOT buying and selling. The chance of you doing both, at the right times, is near zero. Warren Buffett's holding period is "forever." No trading!

4. A **tax-FREE** investment account increases your balance 30%.

5. Putting all your money in one stock or market sector guarantees failure over time. No one investment is perfect. Buy a **group of growing global businesses in a low-cost fund.**

6.   'Dollar cost average' buying technique lowers the cost of shares over time. When you invest a fixed amount each month, you buy more mutual fund shares when the price is low and less when high. Over time, you will own more shares at a lower average cost.

7.   **Consistency** wins over the long term. Quick in and out trading only benefits Wall Street. Market timing may work for a short time but the odds of being right on the buy and sell are long.

8.   **Patience** is required to allow your money to work for you. Building a business takes time. Investing is betting to most of us.

Win the war

With *One Decision*, we can earn 11% on our long-term money and end up with a million dollars or more with one phone call. Now you see how to accumulate more by NOT giving your money to Wall Street. Common sense tells you that those who handle your money are faced with a BIG conflict of interest. How can they earn a living unless they sell products that take your profits.

In my experience, both personal and professional, I find fewer and fewer licensed people who can give ordinary folks the best advice for a set fee like a lawyer. BEST advice: a way to grow our wealth with *no tax and at cost*. We can now earn 10-12% vs. 3.79% on our money. We can now use a proven LONG-TERM strategy so we take advantage of the most powerful investing force —compounding.

Bogle proved cost matters. Buffett proved a simple market index beat the best Wall Street 'fortune tellers.' Senator Roth helped us avoid taxes like the rich. Compounding our assets is the key to wealth; not salespeople.

Fidelity found that the *most successful investors* were those that forgot their account or died. Most wealthy investors have learned that patience is the secret to investing. They see how *costs destroy* their portfolio compounding.

The industry has made building wealth a mystery so it can take $1.3 Trillion from our accounts year after year. The average advisor-run account return was only 3.79%. The fees buy toys for the Pimps of Wall Street. Over time that fee compounds our loss and can take up to 63% of our total *possible* accumulations. Advisors like to buy and sell creating fees for them; taxes for us.

Advisors charge 1-3% whether they beat the averages or not. Advisors don't give refunds! The clear winning strategy is to use one or 10 funds and let compounding work its magic. Over time using a tax-FREE account with low fees, we can accumulate $1,000,000 from $250 a month at 10-12%. Using this calculator moneychimp.com/calculator/compound_interest_calculator.htm, we find the range is 31 to 35 years. If our spouse has an account, we can shorten the time to 26-29 years for a family $1 million.

If we use an advisor, we may give up over $500,000 in total

accumulations. Research has shown that the average investor actually earns just 3.79% not 11% annually over time.

Our funds for building wealth work because they are low-cost strategies inside a unique **tax-FREE trust account.** This eliminates the biggest killers of wealth: TAXES and FEES. We can be our own masters of tax-FREE wealth with patience. There is no need to pick stocks or hire expensive advisors or product pushers with hidden fees. We can do it ourselves as long as we have a plan. The plan is following Warren Buffett's strategy.

One Decision investing is up to you. Advisors can't profit from these steps so you have to call Vanguard or TIAA *yourself* to set up your account. It takes about 1 hour to set up a Roth IRA for each of you. You can do it online or by phone. You can begin with TIAA and $100 automatic contributions or Vanguard with $1,000. Put the contributions on automatic so you don't have to decide every month whether to invest. Future life happens and you want to be spending your $60-80,000 a year not praying Washington won't cut Social Security benefits every year.

If you have been investing, you can convert portions of your IRA each year, paying tax on the earnings as you go. Over time, your Roth account will grow with earnings that are tax-FREE. This money may reduce your overall tax in retirement. It also is a great estate planning tool since no tax will be due from your heirs either.

There is a clear reason why "working millionaires" become wealthy. It is not luck or inheritance. Millions of immigrants to this country have done it before. They lived below their means. They saved and invested in businesses. They did not let temporary cash flow problems stop them from building wealth. They accumulated hard assets and shares of companies and mutual funds.

As many clients say, "I never even miss the contributions because I never see them. Then all of a sudden, I see my statement has $25,000, $50,000, $250,000, $1,000,000, $2,000,000. We are talking real money here."

The real secret to investing is **compounding**. Buffett says:

"My wealth has come from a combination of living in America, some lucky genes, and **compound interest**."

Call Vanguard 800-551-8631 or TIAA **800-223-1200** today.

The Author

Ian Sender has been a financial services executive for over 20 years. He was a managing director of sales units of securities firms. Ian lives in New Jersey and the Caymans. Ian is the author of *The Pimps of Wall Street: You put up the money, take all the risks and we middlemen take 63%*. He is one of the insiders who contributed to the *The Insiders Guides* set of buyers' guides edited by Dan Keppel.

The Insiders' Guides to Buying Discount Financial Services: Buy Direct and Save $3,000 Every Year is available at Amazon, Barnes & Noble, Junglee, bookadda, allbookstores, ebay, fishpond, alibris, powells, booksamillion, etc

The Miracle of Compounding

The best argument we've seen for teaching about finance and the power of compounding is summed up by the table below. These figures are based on an assumed annual rate of return of 10 percent, with no withdrawals and no taxes.

	Example 1:		Example 2:	
Age	Annual Investment	Year-End Value	Annual Investment	Year-End Value
19	$ 2,000	$2,200	$ 0	$ 0
20	$ 2,000	$4,620	$ 0	$ 0
21	$ 2,000	$7,282	$ 0	$ 0
22	$ 2,000	$10,210	$ 0	$ 0
23	$ 2,000	$13,431	$ 0	$ 0
24	$ 2,000	$ 16,974	$ 0	$ 0
25	$ 2,000	$ 20,872	$ 0	$ 0
26	$ 2,000	$ 25,159	$ 0	$ 0
27	$ 0	$ 27,675	$2,000	$2,200
28	$ 0	$ 30,442	$2,000	$4,620
29	$ 0	$33,487	$2,000	$7,282
30	$ 0	$36,835	$2,000	$10,210
31	$ 0	$40,519	$2,000	$13,431
32	$ 0	$44,571	$2,000	$16,974
33	$ 0	$49,028	$2,000	$20,872

34	$0	$53,931	$2,000	$25,159
35	$0	$59,324	$2,000	$29,875
36	$0	$65,256	$2,000	$35,062
37	$0	$71,782	$2,000	$40,769
38	$0	$78,960	$2,000	$47,045
39	$0	$86,856	$2,000	$53,950
40	$0	$95,541	$2,000	$61,545
41	$0	$105,095	$2,000	$69,899
42	$0	$115,605	$2,000	$79,089
43	$0	$127,165	$2,000	$89,198
44	$0	$139,882	$2,000	$100,318
45	$0	$153,870	$2,000	$112,550
46	$0	$169,257	$2,000	$126,005
47	$0	$186,183	$2,000	$140,805
48	$0	$204,801	$2,000	$157,086
49	$0	$225,281	$2,000	$174,995
50	$0	$247,809	$2,000	$194,694
51	$0	$272,590	$2,000	$216,364
52	$0	$299,849	$2,000	$240,200
53	$0	$329,834	$2,000	$266,420
54	$0	$362,818	$2,000	$295,262

55	$ 0	$399,100	$2,000	$326,988
56	$ 0	$439,010	$2,000	$361,887
57	$ 0	$482,910	$2,000	$400,276
58	$ 0	$531,202	$2,000	$442,503
59	$ 0	$584,322	$2,000	$488,953
60	$ 0	$642,754	$2,000	$540,049
61	$ 0	$707,029	$2,000	$596,254
62	$ 0	$777,732	$2,000	$658,079
63	$ 0	$855,505	$2,000	$726,087
64	$ 0	$941,056	$2,000	$800,896
65	$ 0	**$1,035,161**	$,2000	**$883,185**
Less $ invested		($16,000)		($78,000)
		$1,019,161		$805,185
Money increased		64 fold		10 fold

http://www.saferchild.org/power/ It is TIME not timing markets: Everyone has their time.

Your Investment Plan

$250 per month invested automatically in the Vanguard 500 Index:

Year 1	$3000	$ 3,000
Year 5	$3000	$ 20,061
Year 10	$3000	$ 54,746
Year 20	$3000	$ 218,393
Year 30	$3000	$ 707,556
Year 40	$3000	$2,169,740

*Assumes 11% per year with no taxes, no loans or withdrawals or interruptions.

Time value of money: compound interest.
http://www.moneychimp.com/calculator/compound_interest_calculator.htm

Low-cost stock mutual funds

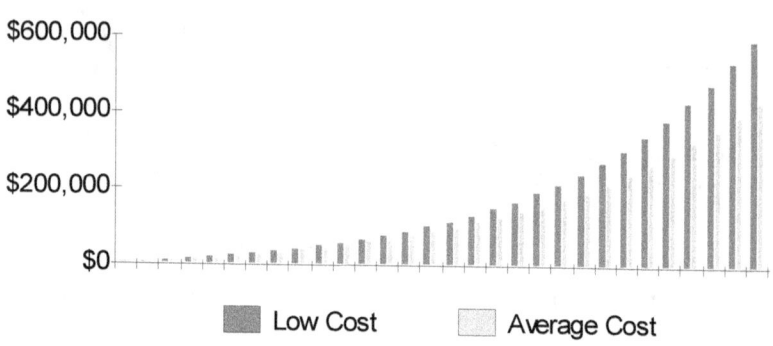

Cost Matters: 0.19% v 1.68%

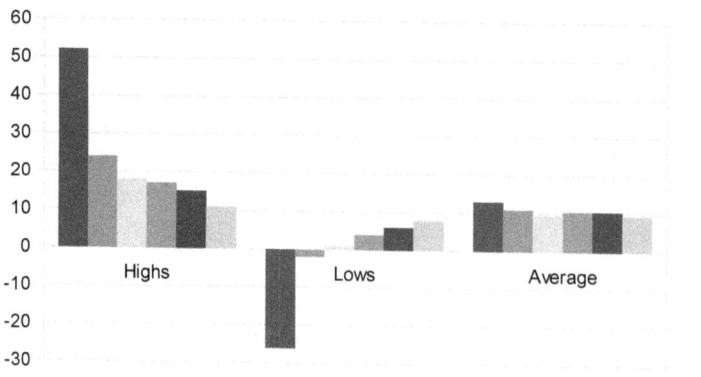

Range of annual returns of stocks, 1950 – 2000

Warren Buffett's Secret

Compounding

Monthly	Accumulation at 12% per year								
	5	10	15	20	25	30	35	40	45	50
$100	$8,167	$23,004	$49,958	$98,925	$187,884	$349,496	$643,095	$1,176,477	$2,145,469	$3,905,834
$200	$16,334	$46,008	$99,916	$197,850	$375,768	$698,992	$1,286,190	$2,352,954	$4,290,938	$7,811,668
$300	$24,501	$69,012	$149,874	$296,775	$563,652	$1,048,488	$1,929,285	$3,529,431	$6,436,408	$11,717,502
$500	$40,835	$115,020	$249,790	$494,625	$939,420	$1,747,480	$3,215,475	$5,882,385	$10,727,346	$19,529,169

You must be vigilant!

It is your money to lose. Ask questions.

Get answers in writing.

Here is your checklist:

1. BrokerCheck and other sources like investor.gov.
2. confirm the salesperson has authorization to trade for you.
3. when you have a question, write to your branch compliance officer OSJ Office of Supervisory Jurisdiction.
4. unregistered offerings are putting your money at risk. CUSIP.
5. are the investment returns within a reasonable range? 2% is the return of US bonds; 11% is the return of the broad market. Here are the 20 year returns of specific market sectors.
12. is the advisor recommending some plan that is illegal? This may require an attorney to check out the deal. Google it.
13. Do you completely understand the terms of the deal and what can go wrong? Assumptions change over time. Sellers leave.
14. Make sure you read the SEC warning about variable annuities.
15. Be wary of free dinners, fine talk, great facilities, cool charts: don't stop doing your homework!
16. Any promised returns, "guarantee" or "safe"? Call the OSJ.
17. Beware: Penny stock (less $2) trading is dangerous for client.